The p
guide to…

DEPUTY HEADSHIP

Lynn Cousins

pfp, London

First published in Great Britain in 1996 by
pfp
61 Gray's Inn Road
London WC1X 8TL

Printed in the UK

ISBN 1 874050 29 5

A catalogue record for this book is available from the British Library.

Contents

Introduction *iv*

1 Why do schools need deputy heads? 1

2 Roles and responsibilities 6

3 Working with the head 15

4 Building professional relationships 21

5 The qualities of a deputy head and how to acquire them 31

6 Developing your role as a deputy head 40

7 Acting headship 49

8 Preparing for headship 54

Conclusion 61

Further reading 62

Index 64

Introduction

This book is a response to the changing role of the deputy head in the primary school.

The 1988 Education Reform Act and the introduction of LMS combined to change the role of the primary head. This in turn caused a fairly dramatic change to the role of the deputy head. The deputy could not continue to be merely a senior teacher who could take assembly when the head was out of school. Heads had to change their own perception of the role which their deputy could play in the running and development of the school. Deputies had to be willing to play a much greater part in the senior management structure of the school. This was no longer a role to be carried out by the member of the staff who was the most senior by virtue of age and experience alone.

The role of the deputy head in the nineties carries with it specific expectations and needs particular professional and personal attributes if it is to provide satisfaction to the individual and benefit to the school.

This short book aims to explore the nature of the role of deputy head and the responsibilities which go along with it, to help someone who is thinking about this as a future role to make some informed choices.

It aims to examine the role in a way that will help heads and governors plan for their own deputy head's appointment and professional development.

It also aims to help an existing deputy head plan her own professional development and suggests some strategies for career enhancement.

The first four chapters try to answer some questions

- What does it mean to be a deputy head?
- What is involved in the role?
- What will be expected of you?

and will probably open up many more questions for you to think about.

Having become, or decided that you would like to become, a deputy head you need to plan a programme of personal professional development. Chapters 5 to 8 will help you plan how to acquire the prerequisite skills and attitudes to move into the role, and to work within the role with increasing effectiveness. They also show how you can develop your professional and interpersonal skills so that you can eventually move on from deputy headship into headship.

For ease of reading, all references to teachers, children and parents in this book are female.

Chapter 1

Why do schools need deputy heads?

This chapter looks briefly at the notion of 'the good school' and the part played by the deputy head in creating a 'good school'. The deputy's role is outlined and the question 'do we need a deputy head?' is discussed.

The 'history' of deputy heads

In 1944, the McNair Report recommended that large primary schools should appoint deputy heads. In 1956, the Burnham Report made it mandatory that there should be deputy heads in schools classed as Group 3 or above, and set a standard scale of payment. Between then and 1970 even small schools were obliged to have deputies and the rates of allowances were increased. The 1988 Education Reform Act gave the school governors responsibility for deciding how many staff the school should have, and allowed them to make decisions about payment above a statutory minimum. LMS increased the levels of internal management responsibility and the pressure which goes with it. There is now no longer a mandatory requirement for a school to appoint a deputy head. At the same time, however, the management and leadership demands made on the head have increased.

Building a good school

A good school is an effective school. The education it offers its children promotes high levels of learning through high levels of teaching. It is seen by parents and the local community as a place which produces good results morally and spiritually, as well as academically. It is open and accessible to the community it serves, and provides a 'mutually supportive environment' (Principles of the World Education Fellowship).

Over the years a great deal of research has been carried out to try to define effectiveness and to set a formula for schools to follow. As part of the ILEA Junior School Project Report in 1986, Mortimore identified some key factors which contribute to effective schooling. The first of these is the leadership offered by the head. The second is the involvement of the deputy head in the strategic management of the school. Mortimore found that effectiveness is promoted by the presence of a stable deputy head, who is involved in policy making, and to whom the head has delegated specific areas of responsibility. Pamela Young also described skilful leadership as 'crucial' to an effective school in a chapter in Reynold's book, 'Studying School Effectiveness'.

OFSTED recognises the role of leadership within schools. It is one of eight key attributes listed under the broad heading of 'Management and Administration', with its own evaluation criteria. These include considering the 'vision' and the 'good leadership' of the governors, the head and the senior staff.

The vision for the school will be, essentially, the head's. At interview she will have put forward a vision for the future of the school which will have been matched, or accepted by the governors as the way forward for that school.

Leadership will be a shared responsibility. It will be delegated by the head and the governors so that the vision can become a reality. Research would seem to suggest that in creating effective leadership the head and the deputy each have an important part to play, but that each depends on the other to fulfil some of their roles. The quality of leadership will be seen in the day-to-day running of the school, in the focus of direction in all that goes on within the school and in the degree of involvement felt by the staff and the parents.

Managing without a deputy head

Traditionally, small schools worked without a deputy head, expecting the most senior of any other teachers on the staff to fill the role as and when necessary. This accounts only for the deputising side of the role of the deputy head.

When LMS gave financial responsibilities to schools, it also gave them the power to choose how that money would be spent. Faced with difficult budget-setting decisions schools could choose to work without a deputy head.

Let us consider the possible scenario when the deputy head has left to take up a new appointment and the governors are having difficulty in setting a legal budget. They may consider not filling the post of deputy head, but securing the responsibilities of the post in other ways. For example, they might

- give two existing members of staff an extra point each on the pay-spine to share the responsibilities of a deputy head, or
- offer the responsibilities of deputy headship and commensurate pay to other staff members on a short-term basis, as a rolling programme.

Potential benefits

- This would be cheaper than employing a deputy head.
- It would offer professional development to more staff.
- It would share the burden of responsibilities more evenly.
- The school could benefit from the expertise and vision of a wider range of people.

Potential problems

- With only a short-term commitment from the individuals involved, the school may not get value for its money.
- There would be a lack of continuity for the school's overall development.
- Research has found that frequent changes of deputy head have a negative effect on the effectiveness of the school.
- The head would spend too much time training or inducting new people to the post and so lose time which should be devoted to other forms of school development.

Points for consideration

- Embodied within the conditions of service for the deputy head is a requirement that she will undertake the professional duties of the head teacher when requested and work alongside the head in the management of the school.
- Mainscale teachers are entitled to a break in the middle of the day and are not expected to carry out any duties during this time. The deputy is entitled to a break as near as possible to the middle of the day, but is expected to return to duty whenever she is needed.

- Mainscale teachers are required to work for 1,265 hours over 195 schooldays. The deputy, like the head, is exempt from this time limit. Deputies and heads must work for as long as is necessary to run the school efficiently.
- Could mainscale teachers be expected to work in a way that is contrary to their Pay and Conditions of Service agreement? Would they be willing to do so? If not, what are the implications for the head's workload? These practical issues should be carefully examined and advice taken from professional bodies by any head or governing body contemplating such a move.

Should a school manage without a deputy?

The role of the deputy embodies within it the concept of the 'trainee head'. A properly managed and well thought out professional development programme enables the deputy to start building up the bank of skills necessary for headship. Experience during the time of deputy headship is vital to the development of interpersonal skills, management techniques and whole-school perspectives. If this opportunity is removed, new heads may in future take up posts for which they have had no real training and end up finding they are are neither happy in the role nor suited to it.

Chapter 2

Roles and responsibilities

This chapter looks at who should be involved in setting the areas of responsibility and specifying the nature of the deputy's role, and offers some ways of approaching the task. It includes an example of a job specification.

Articles or studies investigating the position of the deputy head in the primary school seem to come to the same conclusion: there is no definitive role; but there are plenty of descriptions such as 'hazy', 'uncertain', 'lacking clarity' and 'lacking definition'. The 1988 Education Reform Act and the introduction of LMS may have changed the management structure and raised expectations of increased responsibility for the deputy, but the reality is that the role of the deputy head is still firmly in the hands of individual heads and does not achieve national uniformity.

The main elements of deputy headship

The role of deputy head has two elements, one of deputising for the head and the other of assisting the head.

To deputise

It is expected that the deputy head will be able to 'undertake...the professional duties of the head teacher in the event of her absence from the school' (School Teachers' Pay and Conditions Document). This absence may be planned or it may be unexpected, and it can be for varying lengths of time. The deputy should therefore have a working knowledge of the day-to-day running of the school to maintain the status quo in the short term. Only when the head and deputy have worked together, planning for school development, monitoring the budget and sharing information can the deputy truly deputise in the head's absence. An informed deputy can take the school on, along prescribed paths, continuing the development envisaged by the head.

Deputising for the head in the long term, usually referred to as acting for the head, is dealt with in Chapter 7, as it has constraints and implications beyond the daily role of the deputy head.

To assist

The other – and possibly more substantive – element of the role requires the deputy to work with the head to create a sound management structure. From this will come the crucial framework of leadership necessary to create and run an effective school.

Working alongside the head, the deputy should be able to

- prepare and implement policies and strategic plans
- provide curriculum development
- offer professional development to other staff
- interview and appoint staff at all levels
- be a source of pastoral care throughout the whole school community.

What is special about this role?

Even when the school staff work effectively as a team with a strong sense of cooperation, two major elements are involved. One side deals with the management of the whole school and the other is focussed on daily life in the classroom.

The deputy is the member of staff who has an intimate knowledge of both of these elements.

As a class teacher she knows from first-hand experience the strains and pressures of the teacher's everyday work, whether in delivering the National Curriculum or carrying out testing, compiling records or writing reports. She is in the staffroom and privy to conversations, public or confidential. She is the listening ear on the staff's behalf and possibly the appointed delegate for action.

At the same time she is an integral part of the management structure of the school. She has a whole-school view of finances. She may be aware of restraints which may be needed. She may know facts not yet generally made public.

The skill of the role is to know when to listen, when to speak and when to act; and when not to do any of these things.

This is a time to learn the skills of leadership through example and experiment. With a supportive head and a well-planned professional development programme, it is a time to grow in expertise and confidence. And it is a time to use such authority as is given, to motivate the people who work and learn in the school, to manage change effectively and to contribute to the development of the school.

Who defines the precise role of the deputy in a school?

When a school is about to appoint a new deputy, there should be consultation between the head and the governors to determine what sort of person they are looking for, in terms of both personality and professional expertise. From this, they will be able to draw up a person specification.

It is also useful for the head and deputy to follow a similar exercise to up-date and redefine the role. This could be part of the deputy's appraisal.

Some points to consider during these discussions should include:

The needs of the school

- What are the curriculum strengths of the existing staff?
- Is there a particular area of the curriculum which needs some major input or change?
- In which Key Stage does the school need some management strength?
- Are age or experience a matter of concern?
- Does there need to be a better balance of age or experience within all or part of the school?

The school development plan

- With regard to areas earmarked for development in the medium term (perhaps within the next two years) is there a particular focus or personal strength not already available from existing staff?

- Is there some area of concern which has been left low on the list of priorities because of lack of human resources, but which should be raised if at all possible?

The philosophies and management style of the head

Is the school looking for someone who will

- complement the head, in terms of professionalism and style?
- build in an element of friction, to encourage discussion and debate?
- bring to the school fresh attitudes, a different perspective on management, to add to the current system?
- have the professional competencies to supplement the head's expertise and so create a balance of experience?
- share the same attitudes, management styles and professionalism in order to strengthen an agreed approach?

The prospective deputy's background

- Does the school want someone with a proven track record in a similar post?
- Is the school looking for a first-time deputy who can be trained to suit the school's needs?

The answers to these questions will guide the writing of the job advertisement and the short-listing of the candidates. Once appointed, the voice of the deputy can be added to those determining the precise structure of the role and the level(s) of responsibility.

Establishing the role

To make it realistic the following factors should be taken into account when planning the role.

The past experience of the deputy

If this is a first appointment, the role may well start off with organisational responsibilities, drawing up duty lists and allocating use of shared spaces in the school. This serves to initiate the deputy into the systems current in the school and raises awareness of using staff and facilities fairly but efficiently.

An experienced deputy will have skills to bring to the school. These should be identified through discussion, and a suitable role set up to maximise their use.

The teaching commitment

If a deputy has a full-time teaching commitment she will have limited opportunities for observing the head at work and sharing in the managerial tasks involved in the day-to-day running of the school. In one study (reported in 1993) the majority of deputy heads surveyed agreed with the statement that 'full-time teaching weakens the instrumental role of the deputy head'. Serious thought needs to be given to this problem when planning the deputy's role. The deputy should be allowed time to fulfil the managerial side of the role.

Full-time teaching needs a full-time commitment. The other aspects of the role of deputy head are thereby likely to become added extras, to be done in personal time, or to be neglected in favour of the children. This would be a cause of stress for the individual concerned and a waste of the human resources for which the school is paying. In this event, the deputy is, in effect, little more than a senior teacher to whom the head passes on information.

The deputy also needs to be seen as an exemplar teacher by her colleagues. Part of the role may be to act as an agent for change, through active means or purely by example. As such, the teaching commitment assumes a new dimension whereby the deputy fluctuates between being a teacher and a manager.

Keep it adaptable

The written description of the role and the responsibilities of the deputy head should not be too prescriptive. There should be room for personal and professional development. There should also be room for her to introduce changes in the school.

Allow for professional development

The role as set up in the early stages following appointment should be flexible enough to respond to the growing competencies of the deputy. A pattern for professional development should be set and a structure of expected progression identified. This can then be used to increase, through an agreed strategy, the responsibilities held and discharged by the deputy.

Allow for changes within the school

Changes of staff may alter the balance of professional strength. Budget changes could have a dramatic effect on the priorities set in the school development plan, for better or worse. Some changes may already be planned for within the school development plan.

A well thought out, open-ended job specification for the deputy head will take these changes into account and enable maximum use of this important resource. Following discussion of these points, one school developed the following job description.

A sample job description for a deputy head

Curriculum management

- Play a significant role in the development of the ethos and philosophy of the school by assisting the head in identifying and determining overall aims and objectives.
- Promote the development of a caring atmosphere in which children may develop socially, emotionally, physically, spiritually and intellectually to their full potential.
- Act as curriculum coordinator throughout the school and assist in the development of a broad and balanced curriculum relevant to the needs and stages of development of the children.
- Offer curriculum strengths and be responsible for the organisation and management of policies and resources in curriculum areas.
- Compile standards, achievements and evaluations.
- Organise annual reports and twice yearly interviews with parents.

Leadership and professional development

- Deputise for the head when required and be responsible for staff duties and timetables of shared areas.
- Exercise qualities of leadership, designed to foster co-operation amongst staff.
- Motivate staff and pupils by personal influence and harness expertise for the benefit of the children's learning and experience.

- Plan, implement and evaluate INSET programme.
- Carry out appraisal and set an appraisal programme.
- Establish effective and efficient channels of communication with colleagues and professional support agencies.
- Be aware of the overall needs of the school in terms of resources, premises and staffing, and make appropriate recommendations to officers of the authority for improving the status quo.
- Help to resolve misunderstandings and problems, should they arise, by negotiation.
- Implement the school's policy for behaviour and discipline.

Accountability

- Actively promote and develop liaison with other schools in the area.
- Represent the school in the local community and with appropriate agencies.
- Involve parents in school activities and, through presentations, explain the aims of the curriculum and methods of working.
- Advise and assist the governors in the functioning of the whole school at governors' meetings.
- Be a point of reference for the financial and curriculum sub-groups of the governors.
- With the head be responsible for the financial management of the day-to-day running of the school.

(With thanks to Brackley C.E. Junior School)

Chapter 3

Working with the head

This chapter suggests some ways of creating a head/deputy head partnership which will enhance the effectiveness of both.

Whether standing in for the head or assisting the head, the deputy needs to know what she may or may not do. The understanding of these limits, and their extent, result from the development of an agreed partnership between the head and the deputy, a partnership which is created and developed during the times spent working together. This working partnership should be structured and dynamic.

A structured, dynamic partnership enables the deputy to function as an assistant to the head and thus be a deputy for the whole school, with an influential part to play in its development. As an assistant, the deputy can influence the vision of the school's future as well as the route, pace and content of the process.

A structured partnership

Structure suggests a framework of planning, expectations, success criteria and agreed role definitions. Building the structure demands cooperation and the inter-play of the two personalities concerned.

Planning

Planning needs time and discussion. The roles each will play and the levels of responsibility each will assume need to be planned. You also need to plan for periodic reviews of these elements. The amount of authority handed over to the deputy also needs to be planned. Initially, the head may choose to keep all authority, but there could be a planned approach to the gradual and eventual devolvement of some of that authority. This plan may be based on a time scale, although it is probably more efficient to adopt skills-based criteria.

Expectations

Each person within a partnership will have spoken and unspoken expectations of the other, in terms of professional and personal support and in terms of carrying out their defined role and responsibilities. In a structured partnership, those expectations can be defined and agreed by each person. By agreeing expectations, roles and responsibilities can be kept within manageable boundaries. Through on-going discussions these boundaries can be adapted to suit changing circumstances. This can include widening boundaries as well as narrowing them. The danger of false expectations is off-set when the channels of communication are kept open.

Success criteria

These go alongside expectations and can be set at the same time. The criteria can be part of the deputy head's professional development programme and could be based on the key skills which are examined in Chapter 6. Less important than the actual criteria chosen is the act of choosing. Sitting down together, discussing the possible ways in which they can observe, measure and evaluate success will help the head and deputy to forge a closer working relationship and start to create a shared vision of the school's mission.

Role definitions

Expectations and role definitions are intertwined. Setting up a role carries with it expectations of the person's abilities as well as commitment. There are a number of key roles carried out by the person or people managing the school. Some of these will be the responsibility of the deputy head, others will be carried out by the head. It may be that some of them are shared or they may occasionally be redistributed. These key roles are detailed by other writers from different perspectives.

P. Whitaker (1983) categorises them as

- authority and responsibility
- curriculum
- organisation
- people.

Neville West (1992) offers seven key areas of management, namely:

- teaching and learning
- staff development
- resources and finance
- review, monitoring and evaluation
- external relations
- policies and relevant structures
- professional development.

As with setting criteria for success, sorting out role definitions and examining the needs of the school and the strengths of the partners in this relationship are of intrinsic value. There is a need to keep the roles flexible, for example, in terms of whether a particular area should forever be the province of the head. There may be an obvious division of labour based on the skills of the people concerned and their other commitments in the school, but there should be an opportunity for the one with the skill to allow the other to acquire that skill through supported responsibility.

Role definitions will depend on the strengths and talents of each individual and their level of expertise. Discussions at the time of appointment will have established roles, but it is important to keep them under review. The needs of the school may change.

The skills and levels of expertise of the deputy should grow

In this structured partnership, the framework will be flexible enough to allow for gradual changes, so that the skills of each person can be used to maximum effect for the school and so that professional development can take place. A framework that is too rigid will inhibit the growth of those it contains, depriving them of stimulation and vitality and reducing them to functional beings.

A dynamic partnership

A dynamic partnership provides the meat to flesh out the bones of the structure. It is an ever-changing structure, built on the professional relationship of the head and the deputy.

The partnership needs to be dynamic in the sense of being a changing partnership, reacting to its surroundings and circumstances.

Those in the partnership need to maintain a relationship which permits change, and must be able to move freely within their defined roles in response to circumstantial or developmental needs.

J. Nias (1987) examined one such partnership in her study *One finger, one thumb* and likened it to the way the finger and thumb each has its purpose, but together they can vastly extend their range of functional use. She found two people working together, interchanging roles and thus promoting the efficient running of their school. Underpinning the partnership was a level of communication which enabled each to trust the other, acknowledging each other's place within the system and knowing the boundaries of authority.

It also needs to be a partnership which acts as a dynamic force, causing change and movement around it.

When the head and the deputy are seen to work cooperatively, sharing a common vision for the school, it encourages other members of the staff to behave in a similar way creating what has been described as a 'culture of collaboration' (P. Holly and G. Southworth, 1989). This partnership can be extended through the hierarchy of the system in larger schools, starting with subject coordinators and team leaders, and gradually extending to others who work in the school.

The strength of the partnership built by the head and the deputy is of prime importance to the effectiveness of the school.

- It affects the professional development of all who work in the school.
- It enables the deputy to stand in for the head whenever necessary and to continue to run the school according to the head's vision.

- It allows for the professional development of the deputy to a point where she is ready to accept the more senior position for herself and has the budding expertise to fulfil that role.

Chapter 4

Building professional relationships

This chapter is about the different relationships which you will develop in response to the different aspects of the role.

During the working day, you are likely to have to deal with a wide range of people: children, colleagues, both teaching and non-teaching, other professionals, parents, governors, inspectors, LEA officials, trades people, company reps. The different working relationships you will have with them will be based partly on their expectations of you as the deputy head of the school and partly on the role you are fulfilling at that time – colleague, deputy head or acting head.

In whatever capacity you are working and whoever you are dealing with, you should strive to maintain three key principles.

The deputy should

- demonstrate credibility in professional matters
- maintain confidentiality at all times
- behave in a manner which engenders confidence in her skills.

These are pertinent to all teachers but when exhibited by the deputy gain an added dimension. They are noted by a wider, more public, audience and can be interpreted as being symbolic of what the school, as a whole, stands for.

Relationships with teaching staff

Although you will be working as a colleague with the other teaching staff, as a deputy head you are, in professional terms, their senior. You have responsibilities towards them and, at times, for them. You are one of them, but there are times when you must stand apart.

As a colleague: a relationship based on respect and credibility

The deputy head needs to earn the respect of other staff members. This is initially achieved by the quality of your classroom practice. As fellow professionals, the rest of the staff will appreciate the effort and skill needed to maintain an effective classroom, but they won't be hoodwinked by superficialities.

With respect comes credibility. Without respect as a teacher you will find it difficult to achieve credibility when acting as deputy.

As a counsellor: a relationship based on trust and confidentiality

The deputy head plays a major part in the emotional and social well-being of the staff. Confidentiality is a crucial matter within this sort of relationship and is discussed in more detail on page 44.

Teachers may bring their problems to you simply to unburden themselves. Talking through a problem, or letting someone with authority know about difficult or uncomfortable situations can be sufficient to take the pressure off.

This tactic may be used by staff who don't want to make a formal complaint, but would actually like you to decide to do something about the situation for them.

In fact the person using you as a counsellor is just as likely to be the head as a class teacher, and this role is examined in the chapter on working with the head (Chapter 3).

As a facilitator of professional development: a relationship based on integrity, trust and sensitivity

Professional development takes place in a variety of ways and with different levels of intensity. Here are four possible situations in which you can be actively involved, as deputy, in the professional development of your colleagues:

- unplanned moments when questions or discussions will arise which will allow you to pass on advice or offer suggestions
- pre-planned INSET training sessions
- the appraisal process
- as a mentor to newly-qualified teachers.

Unplanned opportunities

Once your professional integrity has been established in the minds of the staff, they may bring you their professional problems. Use these opportunities to encourage your colleague to think through the problem and test out her own conclusions. Don't set yourself up as the fount of all knowledge, however, feeling obliged to provide a panacea for all situations. If you point someone in the direction of the answer, they are more likely to use it and learn from the experience.

You may also find it necessary to set up informal discussions which lead a colleague to question her own practice. Some people are not aware of errors or misjudgements in their classroom practice and will need to be guided to see this before you can help them to set things right. This will call for considerable tact on your part if you are to move someone forward professionally without belittling them or destroying their confidence.

INSET arrangements

As a deputy you may be expected to take responsibility for the school's INSET arrangements. This involves some degree of budget planning as well as knowledge about the needs of the school and the professional needs and aspirations of the individual teachers. These are not necessarily the same thing and it needs diplomatic handling on occasions to move colleagues in the most appropriate direction. You can expect to have to negotiate with staff in order to provide INSET without overspending the supply budget. And you will need to encourage individual members of staff to follow the most appropriate form of training for their own professional development, and to promote courses and training, which can later be shared with the rest of the staff, in order to further whole-school development.

INSET can also take the form of school-based, in-house sessions. You should be able to set up and run some of these.

To plan such sessions you will need to be forward thinking. Within the framework of the school development plan the deputy should be able to

- identify areas of need amongst the staff's strengths,
- think about the needs of the school, and
- know what is available, affordable and manageable.

Setting up such sessions does not mean that you should be the sole provider or leader, but you should, as the saying goes, 'know a man who can...'. By encouraging participation by other members of staff, allowing them to share their skills and knowledge with their colleagues, you can provide them with opportunities to enhance their own professional development.

Appraisal

In many schools, it is likely that the deputy will play a part in the appraisal process. This is a new role for which LEAs are providing their own training programmes. It allows scope for a greater level of professional trust to be built up when it is handled sensitively. As an appraiser of one of your colleagues, you can use the opportunity to build a relationship which is totally confidential, gain an insight into your colleague's professional aspirations and play a direct part in her ongoing development programme.

As a mentor

This term is used formally in school to mean the teacher with responsibility for any newly qualified teachers on the staff, but it is also an important part of the relationship between the deputy head and her colleagues. Younger teachers, teachers new to the school and teachers returning after an absence, all benefit from the support of another teacher, if only to help them find their way round the resource areas. Many will also need the advice, the positive feed-back and the listening ear of a supportive deputy head. Make time to go into the classroom, when the 'new' member of staff is teaching, and at the beginning or end of the school day, to see that everything is going well for them. It can also be helpful to make sure that they have someone to speak to in the staffroom at break times.

Relationships with non-teaching staff

In many ways these relationships are similar to those which you will have with the teaching staff. You need to be their colleague, their counsellor and their mentor.

Communicating with non-teaching staff provides good professional development for the deputy head. If a head will hand over to you the responsibility for the deployment and training of these members of staff, you can gain valuable experience of managing people, whilst making them feel that they have an effective part to play in the school. With the responsibility, the head must also hand over authority. You will need to feel and to know that you are in charge. You will need to be seen to be exercising authority, and that authority, and any decisions you make, need to be respected publicly by the head.

With regard to professional development, however, contracts for non-teaching staff do not usually have built into them an expectation of further training, nor does this appear in the budget. The school's lunch-time supervisors and, if schools are fortunate enough to be able to employ them, non-teaching classroom assistants, welfare assistants or special needs assistants, are normally paid only for the hours that they work. Any professional training therefore is voluntary on their part.

The most accessible way to provide some professional development for non-teaching staff is through school-based sessions. These can be aimed specifically at the identified needs of the individuals and held at convenient times.

You could invite these members of staff to appropriate staff meetings or set up some meetings especially for them, as opportunities to voice their opinions and make their requests known. Be sure to listen to what they have to say and take notice of their opinions.

If they are treated with respect and trust, and helped to see their role within the school as one which is positive and appreciated, then they are more likely to become keen to learn more and to develop the skills which will make them more effective.

Relationships with visitors to the school

When the head is in school you will probably not be expected to deal with visitors in general. But there will be times when the head is already engaged or is out of school, and at such times you will need to receive people who come into the school.

When people are expected, it is likely that the head will have discussed with you the approach to be taken or the information to be sought or given. But when the visitor is unannounced, you will need to be aware of the boundaries within which you are allowed to act. When you and the head have worked closely together, discussing issues of procedure and sharing the vision for the school's development, you will have developed an empathetic awareness of these boundaries. As you gain experience, there will be less need on the head's part to lay down strict guidelines every time she leaves the premises. The sensitive deputy will have sufficient professional integrity to deal with matters in an authoritative way without treading on anyone's toes, knowing when to make a decision and when to defer the matter. When a head trusts her deputy, having provided training through discussion, example and experience, and has handed over the authority needed to carry out the given duties, the deputy is able to gain real experience of acting as a head, making decisions and accepting the consequences. All types of people visiting the school are then able to conduct their business in the knowledge that matters will be dealt with efficiently.

Relationships with governors

The deputy head needs to have a background knowledge of how the governors work and their role within the school and needs to be able to deputise for the head on occasions.

As the governors have appointed you as the deputy they will need to see evidence that you are a suitable person for the role.

You also need to be cognisant with the workings of the governors. In addition to reading the minutes of the meetings and having verbal feedback, you should should take advantage of any opportunity to be present at the meetings. On appointment you may be invited to attend as an observer. You may be given the chance to be elected as a full voting member, either as a teachers' representative or as a coopted member. Take these opportunities as they provide a means of gaining an insight into the running of the whole school.

If the head is absent from the school for any length of time, it is possible that you would need to take over the head's role with the governors, including taking part in a governors' meeting.

If the governors are to feel confident that the school can be safely left in your hands, you must show that you are not only aware of things going on in the school, but also have a clear picture of where the school is going and of the mechanisms which enable those things to happen. All of this grows out of good team work with the head, of continued sharing of ideals, plans and actions. With this kind of background knowledge, you will be able to step into the head's role in a governors' meeting and maintain continuity for the school, whilst providing evidence to the governors that they can trust you professionally.

Relationships with the children

For many children the deputy head, if even recognised as such, is the person who takes assembly when the head is out of school. There needs to be a clearly defined role for the deputy head to play in terms of dealing with children, if they are to give due regard to the person or the position.

As a counsellor

Frequently, the deputy head has responsibility for children with special needs, which may be learning, emotional or behavioural. These children and their parents can build up a close relationship with the deputy head and through word of mouth, in the community or at the school gate, the deputy can gain a reputation for being someone to turn to when parents need advice or support. Sensitivity and confidentiality will earn respect and trust, and the general goodwill of the parents. The children, too, may begin to see the deputy as a caring and trustworthy person.

As an arbiter

Each school has its own behaviour management structure, often with a hierarchy of seriousness. From the class teacher the more serious or persistent offences may pass to the year group or team leader, and from there to the deputy head before the ultimate sanction of the head. When children are aware of this pattern and see it operating in a consistent manner, it helps them to identify the scale of their misdemeanour.

Whatever the system within a school the deputy needs to be seen to be acting fairly, taking note of all sides of the argument and not undermining other staff or pre-empting the stance which the head will take. The deputy may also be doing this whilst her own class watches! Be professional, cool, calm and collected and save your loudest voice and sternest manner until there is nothing else you can do. Don't immediately threaten the child with the head as that will undermine your own position. Act on your own behalf. Only when all you can do fails, should you suggest to the person who sent the child to you that the child should now be sent to the head.

Whatever the child has done and whatever sanction you mete out to her, the child should respect you for your fairness. A sense of justice is strong in most children's minds.

In conclusion

The quality and type of the relationships which the deputy head will build up depend upon two factors. One is the role of the deputy as defined within the school. The other is the deputy's personality.

The development of these relationships is an integral part of the deputy's on-going professional development. The chance to build sound relationships promotes a sense of self-esteem in the individual as well as enhancing the deputy in the eyes of other people.

As part of the planned professional development programme for the deputy there should be experiences and opportunities to acquire and practise these skills.

Chapter 5

The qualities of a deputy head and how to acquire them

Curriculum vitae

The CV which you will send off with your application for a post as a deputy head is a summary of your educational and professional development. When compiling a CV, there is always a danger of missing out vital details or of not being able to find or remember the exact title of some course you went on a few years earlier.

Think of your CV as a diary of your professional development. Start it as soon as you can in your career. The advent of appraisal has given a degree of focus to this activity. Some newly qualified teachers started building up just such a professional profile even during their training. It is a good discipline to try to maintain it. It needs only a loose-leaf file or ring binder to begin to make a record of your progress. Keep in it

- appraisal records
- notes and handouts from courses you attend
- notes from training sessions undertaken in your staff meetings
- copies of your job descriptions.

If you are asked to take on any other responsibilities, organising the school's harvest or Christmas production, for example, make a note of it, with dates and possibly a quick note of the skills you acquired through this experience. Add it to your file.

When you come to write your CV you will then have a complete record, from which you can pick the information which is most relevant to the post for which you are applying.

Professional experience

A wide range of experience gives you a broad picture of education. The opportunity to work in different kinds of schools should be welcomed. The process of teaching varies and can depend upon the size of the school and the nature of the catchment area. Try to gain experience across a range of schools, if that is at all possible, because breadth of experience is as important as length.

It is also important to try to gain experience of teaching as many different age groups of children as possible. You will have a greater understanding of your school, and the staff in it, if you can empathise with the pressures and the rewards of teaching children of different ages.

A third area in which you will benefit from a breadth of experience is that of curriculum expertise. Taking responsibility for different areas of the curriculum, following INSET courses and reading educational literature will help to build up your bank of expertise and knowledge.

The professional process

At the start of your teaching career you may not have a clear picture of the path you want to follow. The needs of the school you are in may determine the courses you attend and the skills you practise. If teaching is your second career, you may already have a number of skills under your belt. Circumstances may take you along paths which you had not considered, but which give you a high degree of professional satisfaction. But once you have made the decision to go into school management as your next career move, you can begin to be pro-active in determining for yourself the courses to attend and the training you will embark upon.

The first step is to share this decision with the head and the deputy head of your school. Between them they have the experience to help you move in the right direction and the expertise to advise you of the skills and attitudes you need to gain or refine for school management.

Professional skills

These can be divided into the classroom skills of the practitioner and the academic skills of the educationalist. A delicate balance should be maintained between these two. Each has an equally important role to play, but which will seem to be more important to you will vary according to the different groups of individuals with whom you come into contact.

Classroom practice

The first skill to be acquired – and one which must be clearly demonstrated – is that of being an excellent classroom practitioner. Without this fundamental skill, it will not be possible to earn the respect of your colleagues or maintain professional integrity. As more duties fall onto your shoulders as deputy, preoccupying your mind and sapping energy, the children in your care must continue to receive a first class education.

You must be able to demonstrate

- a sound knowledge of the curriculum
- an ability to motivate children and differentiate their tasks according to their needs
- well planned and prepared teaching
- up-to-date and useful record keeping
- organised and efficient storage and use of resources,

whilst creating an atmosphere in which children can work with confidence, feeling respected and trusted.

Academic development

You will also need to have a sound educational background. For most teachers this is similar up to the time of qualifying. After that, the differences start to appear. You will need to show that you have continued to keep up-to-date with current thinking. Professional papers and books will keep you informed, but you should also take opportunities to discuss issues with your fellow professionals. Not the staffroom chat about how difficult it all is, or discussions of internal matters, but high quality, thoughtful debate on broader issues. Not only will this broaden your own spectrum of thinking and understanding, but it will also help you to construct and deliver meaningful arguments.

One way of achieving this is to attend seminars or conferences whenever possible. Another route which many follow is that of further study. Studying for a diploma or master's degree will provide a network of similarly minded people with whom you can debate current educational trends and their potential implications whilst keeping abreast of new thinking.

Organisational skills

Every teacher benefits from the development of these skills, starting with the basic skills of organising and managing your classroom so that it runs efficiently and effectively.

Resources

As a curriculum coordinator you will gain experience of looking after the resources for use across the whole school. It is possible that you will be given the opportunity to manage a small budget, planning your spending for maximum effect. If so use this opportunity, and any others like it, to increase your skills. Keep up-to-date with new developments and concepts through reading, visiting exhibitions and talking to staff in other schools. Consult your colleagues regularly to find out what they need. Try things out in small ways, or talk to others who may have already bought things, before you commit your budget and your reputation to new products or schemes. Learn to take a calculated risk, but never lose sight of the value of experience.

In time you will need to be able to manage the resources of the whole school, from the buying through to the storage and use, and eventually their replacement for better or different resources.

To manage resources effectively you need to build up

- knowledge of what is available
- an ability to budget and spend wisely according to planned priorities
- a team spirit amongst staff enabling planned and fair sharing of resources
- an attitude amongst staff and pupils which promotes careful and considerate use of resources.

People

As a team leader you can start to develop your interpersonal skills through encouraging your colleagues, supporting them and motivating them to even greater things. These issues are examined in more detail in Chapter 6, 'Developing your role as a deputy head'.

Time

This is one of the most difficult areas to organise and manage. The adage that work will expand to fill the time available is a most apt one in educational establishments. The work you could do will never be completed and will certainly never dry up. To work for the sake of seeming to be busy would be a fruitless exercise. Know what you have to do. Decide on the approximate time needed to complete the whole task or any discrete part of it. When it reaches the top of your list of priorities, do it.

Manage your time, don't be managed by it

Allow time for the unexpected. There will always be someone who needs something doing now, if not yesterday! Rearrange your priorities if possible and be accommodating. (It may be your turn to forget something tomorrow.) This is a good time to practise the art of delegation. You may even have to practise the difficult art of saying 'No'.

Ill-managed time is one of the causes of stress. Give yourself enough time to fulfil your duties properly and then give yourself time for home commitments and recuperation.

The application, the interview and the appointment

Your professional skills and potential will be represented in your application form and your CV. If you have demonstrated a professional attitude and a sense of commitment throughout your career, this will be credited to you in the references from your current and former employers. Your attitude will be seen by others in the way in which you present yourself verbally and in writing to your prospective employers.

Your attitudes towards your prospective role can be judged with reference to

- interpersonal skills, speaking to new people
- personal organisation
- appearance
- relationships with the head
- relationships with all other staff of the school
- relationships with children
- ability to see past the obvious and make professional judgments from your observations.

Remember that your 'interview' starts with the letter you write or the phone call you make when you first enquire about the advertised post. The way you speak to people, the manner of your approach, will give people their first impression of you. One of the things you will be expected to do as a deputy head is to speak to people whom you have never met before. This is your first opportunity to show that you can do this in a calm, professional manner.

Try to visit the school before you apply. Meet the head and make sure that she is the kind of person with whom you could work closely. Yours will be a working relationship which affects the whole school, the staff and the children. It must be built on mutual respect if it is to be successful.

When completing your application form, keep to the point and check your facts before you begin. A neatly written, clean and well-organised application form will be read in a more positive frame of mind by your prospective employers.

Read carefully through the detailed job specification before you write the accompanying letter of application. Make sure you can offer what the school is looking for. Try to respond to the details outlined in the specification and refer to what you have seen and deduced from your preliminary visit.

If you are invited for interview, plan carefully for any presentation required of you. Be sure to be there in good time with all that you need sorted and checked. Schools can't be run efficiently if the staff are not highly organised.

Think carefully about what you will wear. You are hoping to become a member of the senior management team of a professional organisation. You should look the part – smart, efficient but comfortable.

Use any opportunities to look around the school. Talk to all members of the staff, teaching and non-teaching. Find out where the school is in terms of development. Think about what you see and how you could help to move the school onwards. Talk to the children, be interested in all that is going on. How you act and what you say will almost certainly be part of the interview process. Members of staff will be observing your approach to the children and your general manner and disposition, and referring back to the head or other members of the interview panel.

If you are appointed, set up some further visits to the school. Not only do you need to get to know your colleagues and the children you will teach, you also need to start building up your relationship with the head as the senior management team of the school and prepare for the part you will play within it.

Chapter 6

Developing your role as a deputy head

Once you are in the role of deputy head you will continue to develop all of the skills you have previously exhibited as a class teacher or team leader. In addition there are two key elements to add

- you need to develop a whole-school perspective on decision making
- you need to become even more skilful at managing people.

A whole-school perspective

You need to become a school teacher rather than a class teacher. It may be necessary for you to make decisions affecting the whole school and as such you must be aware of the needs of the school in a global rather than a parochial way.

For this to be feasible, you need to have some way of finding out what is happening throughout the whole school and of keeping in touch with all of the age groups.

One way of achieving this is for you to become involved in monitoring standards throughout the school. By going into the different classes for an identified purpose, you will become more aware of the areas of strength as well as of the areas of weakness. You will be able to envisage the whole picture.

Another way of keeping a whole-school perspective on things is through involvement in the school development plan. Before any planning can begin, the senior management of the school and the governors need to agree on the aims of the school. The conditions of service for deputy heads set out that they should 'play a major role' in formulating the aims and objectives of the school. An awareness of the whole school will allow you to contribute effectively to that debate. At the same time, taking part in that debate will help to give meaning to the importance of having this wider perspective always in your consciousness.

As a curriculum coordinator, you should have had experience of developing policies and overseeing their implementation. As the deputy head you need to become involved, with the governors, in writing policies beyond the taught curriculum. Policies relating to concepts such as equal opportunities and behaviour, affect every member of the school and have a definite impact upon the ethos of the school.

Managing finances

It is not generally required of the deputy head that she should have an intimate knowledge of managing the finances of the school. It would, however, seem remiss if opportunities to become acquainted with the financial aspects of LMS were not taken up. At any time, the deputy head could be called upon to act as head and therefore needs some awareness of the systems in place.

The introduction of LMS has changed the role of the head and created a need to know about financial matters. These vary from one authority to another and depend on the size of the school. The school secretary may have a background in book-keeping or accountancy and be able to contribute to the financial running of the school. But you must be able to set budgets, read financial data and keep track of the money in the school's account.

Local authorities provide training (initial and up-dating) to heads and secretaries working for them. Some authorities offer training for deputies. Even if you are not dealing with the budget directly, it is useful to attend such training so that you can familiarise yourself with the language of accounting and learn some of its intricacies.

As a curriculum coordinator or team leader, you may have been given your own budget. This is the beginning of your financial training. Plan your spending. Investigate the value of what you are buying, in terms of both cost and usefulness. Plan for emergencies. Make sure you keep within your budget.

As a deputy, you should be able to work with your head when the budget is being set. At first your role may only be that of observer, but take note of the thinking that goes into the setting of the budget as well as of the practical procedures involved. Progress to a stage where you have thought about issues and plans and can offer suggestions. Accept the head's final word and learn from the discussion about the feasibility of your suggestions. You may be fortunate enough to work with a head who will eventually let you set and control one section of the budget. In these ways you will gradually build up your knowledge and confidence in the financial management of the school.

The LEA and the DfEE

You will need to have a working knowledge of these two institutions if you are called upon to manage the school in the head's absence.

Use all opportunities to find out more about the workings of the LEA. What is it still responsible for? Who is in charge of what? In what circumstances do you need to contact them?

Read DfEE documents which are sent to the school. Become familiar with the legal requirements and obligations of the school. If you are suddenly called upon to act as head of the school, you may need to know any of these things. It will make such times less stressful if you have some knowledge, however limited or vague, to help you cope.

Managing people

At the start of your teaching career, you will have been fine-tuning your interpersonal skills as you related professionally to the children in your class. You learned to handle parents, both formally and informally. You may have been required to work with non-teaching staff as well as your fellow professionals.

As a team leader you should have acquired and developed invaluable skills in leading people, perhaps effecting changes, and offering some degree of professional development.

You may have been able to train as a teacher tutor, working with students from a local college.

You may have acted as a mentor to a newly qualified teacher.

As you move into higher management positions these skills acquire a higher priority and in many cases can become issues in their own right. The ability to handle people sensitively can make or break your career move into senior management.

The particular relationships you create with the people you meet are dealt with in more detail in Chapter 4. This chapter suggests the skills you need to have in order to create and maintain those relationships.

Awareness

Awareness involves getting to know the people with whom you come into contact. As teachers, we all appreciate the difference it makes when a parent tells us of a problem at home which may be affecting the child in some way. We are alerted to the child's behaviour and emotional state, we take a little more care in the way we handle the child, we are better equipped to deal with any outburst or abnormal behaviour shown by that child.

Awareness of a colleague's state of mind, or of the mood that she is in, will similarly help you to respond in appropriate ways. This is not a *carte blanche* for intruding into someone's personal affairs, but a reminder to stop to think before you act or speak, to find out the whole situation before trying to change or condemn something.

Sensitivity

Sensitivity should follow on from awareness. It also includes respect, trust and empathy. Remember the pressures that everyone is under and try not to add to them. Talk to people as you would like to be addressed, without belittling or patronising them. Treat people as responsible adults and they will respond in that way. Treat them as small children and they will possibly live up to (or down to) your expectations of them. Most people will rise to an occasion and respond positively to a well presented challenge.

Sensitivity towards confidentiality is another important aspect of managing people. A confidence given should not be divulged unless it relates to a criminal matter, eg. child abuse, and then you should tell the person that you are obliged to pass on anything she tells you, as soon as you realise what is being said.

In normal circumstances, however, you should keep confidential matters to yourself. If someone hears you passing on confidences, they will think twice about trusting you themselves.

When dealing with people, offer advice if asked and deal with situations when requested. But above all try to listen in a non-critical, non-judgmental way.

Verbal communication

With individuals

Remember that communication is about listening as well as speaking. It is in your facial expressions and your body language.

Find a suitable place and time in which to have any conversation. In some circumstances 'here and now' may be fine, but you may prefer to be more comfortable or more private. Or you may feel the need for a witness to be present. Learn to take charge of the situation and the time and place. If a conversation takes a particular turn, politely but firmly call a halt or suggest a further meeting. Be professional at all times, even under provocation, and *write down details* of the meeting and any follow-up you have agreed to undertake if that is appropriate.

With larger groups of people (eg. parents, governors, INSET sessions)

By nature teachers are communicators. The skills developed in the classroom need to be transferred to a wider audience. This is not as easy as it sounds. Many teachers, who are fully at ease addressing a classroom full of children, become quite nervous if they have to address a room full of adults, be they colleagues or parents.

Prepare for public speaking in the same way that you would prepare for a lesson. Plan what you want to say, how you will approach your subject and for how long you expect to speak. If you speak clearly from brief notes and maintain good eye-contact, you should not encounter any major problems. Following these basic principles will take the edge off your nerves.

Business meetings

Leading staff meetings or chairing committees will definitely be expected of you as a head, and hopefully you will be given these duties as a deputy. Take up any opportunity you are offered to fill these roles. When you are not leading, watch the person who is, note how they handle situations and learn from them.

Written communication

Much of the school's communication with parents will be in the form of letters. These are usually compiled by the head and there may be few opportunities for you to gain practical experience of this at other stages of your career. If such opportunities do arise then consider them seriously and make full use of them.

Points to remember:

Presentation

- Make sure it is attractive, clear and easy to read
- Check your spelling, grammar and punctuation
- Use a word-processor

Contents

- All facts and information should be double-checked for accuracy
- Use short sentences for clarity
- Do not patronise or write down to people
- Be polite, not dogmatic

Key skills

The skills of the deputy head are part of a continuum of skills which develop throughout the career of any teacher. The checklist overleaf accordingly starts with the newly qualified teacher and progresses to the start of headship. It is not a case of acquiring one skill first and then adding another. Rather, it should be seen as a bank of skills being accumulated, starting with the professional skills and then moving on into management skills. Continually you develop existing skills, and widen their range, whilst starting to learn new ones.

Key skills checklist

Professional skills	classroom practice academic development
Organisational skills	resources time
Management skills	people communication finances school

A common element of all of these skills is that the deputy head needs to demonstrate

- an attitude of professional integrity
- an ability to see the whole picture

In addition, you will need

- a sense of humour
- tolerance
- commitment

and someone who can support you when you eventually get home!

Chapter 7

Acting headship

Why should you act as head?

- Because it is an integral part of your role as the head's deputy.
- Because it will give you some idea of what it really means to be the head of a school.
- To advance your own professional development and expertise.
- To demonstrate to others that you can do the job.
- To help you decide upon your next career move.

The time spent as the deputy head of a school will have provided opportunities for professional development. The quality of the work which you have undertaken and the relationships which you have developed will now be key factors influencing your potential success as an acting head.

Establishing contacts

During your time as a deputy it is useful to build up a support system of other professionals.

There will be a named inspector who is responsible for the school. She will be a link between any other services offered by your LEA and the school. This person can play a major part in the development of the school and the people who work in it. Building up a working relationship with the inspector can be beneficial to your own professional development, but it will also prove invaluable if you are ever left to act as head and need some advice or support.

Develop your own network of support through contact with other deputies in the area. Attend meetings which allow you to get to know the other heads in your locality. Use the support of the professional unions. All of these could provide you with much needed and appreciated support if you are faced with a new situation when you are acting as head.

Watch out for information on training schemes, such as 'Headlamp', and the availability of mentoring from your fellow professionals. These will give you a structure around which to build your professional development.

You may be called upon to act as head in a number of different circumstances. The context of each situation will determine the role you will play, the constraints upon you and the potential learning you will gain. Here are three examples.

1 The head may be away because of sickness, but is expected to return, possibly within a term or so.

Your role in these circumstances is to keep the ship afloat. If you have played an active part in the management of the school, you will know what the head had in mind for that term. You will have an understanding of the developments planned and of the strategies which the head would have employed.

Use the time to

- demonstrate your understanding of the routines of school daily management
- show your skills at coping with the unexpected in a cool and professional way

- gain the confidence of your colleagues, the governors and the children and their parents in your ability to manage the school.

Then you can return the school to the head's management knowing that things have continued to move forward as planned, and that you have acquired some useful experience.

2 The head may be filling another post for a whole school year, but is expecting to return to this post.

In these circumstances you can use the time to do more than just maintain the school. Prior to the head's departure, there will have been opportunities for you to work with her and the governors on the school development plan and the parts of it which will be put into place during your time as acting head. It is therefore possible that you will have had some part to play in determining the development of the school for that year.

Before an arrangement of this sort takes place there will have been discussion with the governors about

- your ability to take on this role
- what they will expect of you, and
- the sorts of things which they will allow, or even encourage, you to do.

Once this type of agreement has been reached you should be able to act with confidence as the head of the school.

Use the time to

- demonstrate your ability to participate in the longer term plans for the school
- affect the thinking of the staff, if appropriate

- implement some aspects of the school development plan with the agreement and commitment of the staff and governors.

This will be your first chance to show that you can be a leader as well as a manager. (See Chapter 8 for a broader definition and discussion of these two aspects of the head's role.) Use the time effectively as part of your own professional development programme. But always remember that you will have to hand the role and the responsibilities back. If you keep to the expectations laid down by the governors, within the agreed long-term aspects of the school development plan, you should be able to run the school, and possibly manage some beneficial changes, whilst maintaining the ethos which will allow the head to resume control on her return.

3 For some reason the school may be 'between heads'. You may be acting as head indefinitely, or for a fixed term. You may be planning to apply for the post yourself, or the head may have already been appointed but is not due to take up the post immediately.

If you are awaiting the arrival of a newly appointed head then this is not the time to start making changes on your own initiative.

Meet with the prospective head and share your ideas for the future of the school. Presumably, her ideas and vision will have been shared with, and approved by, the governors during interview. This may be a time simply to maintain the status quo, so that you can hand over a school where things are in order and up-to-date, ready for a new beginning. The new head may, however, have some things which she would personally like you to carry out before she takes up her post.

Use the time to

- set your own professional standard
- demonstrate your ability to manage effectively
- start creating a positive working relationship with your new head.

If you are planning to apply for the post, then this is not a time for simply maintaining things as they are. You will need to make your own mark on the school and its members.

Use the time to

- make some achievable, obvious but non-controversial changes
- take some area of school life which you are certain, through observation and due consultation, is in need of change and start changing it
- demonstrate your ability to see a need and to do something about it.

Chapter 8

Preparing for headship

If you enjoy the role of deputy head and wish to make that the pinnacle of your career, then you should not feel pressured by those around you into thinking that you have not quite made it, or that yours is only a secondary achievement. The role has its own rewards and these are as valuable as you allow them to be. In many ways the role of the deputy in the nineties is not far removed from the role of the head in past years. You may have total responsibility for the curriculum or play a major role in the children's discipline and welfare. You may have a pastoral responsibility for other members of staff as well as for managing their professional development. You may be working in close partnership with the head to increase the effectiveness of your school.

Then again, you may be planning to move on to a new challenge, that of headship. This chapter will suggest some of the preparatory thinking required.

In many ways, preparing for this move is very similar to the way in which you anticipated the move into deputy headship.

You will have continued the preparation and formulation of your CV through planned professional development as a teacher and deputy. That programme will have given you some expertise in the skills you would require as a head, for certainly most are developed from those you have used as a deputy.

Experiences gained from opportunities to act as head will have enabled you to check out your perspectives of the school as a whole and will have tested your professional attitudes.

You should now be giving serious consideration to two key features of headship:

- the style of management you will adopt, and
- the nature of the leadership you will give.

Manager or leader

The leader of any organisation should be a person with vision. The leader needs to be able to picture the situation as it will be in the foreseeable future and know how the organisation aims to get there.

The manager is the person who will effect the changes and developments that enable the vision to become a reality.

A head assumes both roles, being responsible both for creating the vision and making it a reality. However, an effective head delegates authority for both managing and leading, whilst retaining overall responsibility for each of these roles.

The head should have a vision for the future of the school, arising from her analysis of its current position.

The governors and head should create a mission statement together to summarise the essential features of that vision.

All of those involved in the running of the school, the head, the senior management team and the governors, should contribute to setting a school development plan to put it into practice.

As a deputy head you should have experienced both management and leadership at levels delegated to you by the head, suited to the abilities you have demonstrated.

The experience of management and leadership tasks has already been looked at in earlier chapters and will have formed a considerable part of your professional development as a deputy. The question now is, how to analyse and develop your management and leadership abilities.

Management abilities

As a head, the day-to-day running of the school will be your responsibility. The way you manage that task will depend upon certain contributory factors, eg. your own personality, any teaching commitment you may have, the experience and abilities of the staff, your relationship with the governors and the amount of secretarial time available. Each of these factors demands its own particular management ability.

Your own personality

- You need to be able to keep calm, anticipate and plan for events. Crisis management is only for crises.
- You need to be able to negotiate, consult and co-ordinate with others.
- Dictatorship is not an acceptable form of school management.

Your teaching commitment

- You need to have your time well planned and you need to be organised.

- You need to be able to focus on the particular role you are playing. There may be times when your teaching is interrupted. Have strategies for these occasions.

The staff, their experience and their abilities

- You need to delegate responsibility and authority to members of staff and trust them to carry them out professionally and according to the agreed ethos and principles of the school.

The governors

- You need to be able to communicate effectively with the governors and to reach agreement on the delegation of responsibility for the management of the school.

Secretarial support, time and expertise

- You need to delegate appropriate responsibilities to these members of staff to give you the time to deal with other tasks.

Leadership abilities

As a head, you will be leading the school towards the vision of the school's future position, trying to achieve the school's mission statement. Others will be sharing this leadership with you, each taking responsibility for some of the planned developments. For, to be effective, leadership should be sufficiently flexible to be shared by the group. As a head you will carry the ultimate responsibility for the actions and results of others and so you will need to delegate wisely and monitor developments.

JAF Stoner and RE Freeman (1989) describe leadership as the process of directing and influencing the task-related activities of the members of the group. You will need to develop particular abilities if you are to become an effective leader. You should

- have a clear sense of direction
- communicate with enthusiasm to inspire others
- listen and respond in a constructive way to the ideas and experiences of others
- be prepared to adopt changes
- manage change in a positive way.

A clear sense of direction comes from knowing your situation and the players in it. It comes from considered discussions and an ability to think through the possibilities, weighing the alternatives and balancing idealism against reality. It comes from confidence in your own ability to recognise the potential around you.

With this confidence will come an enthusiasm for the projected achievements of the school. The ability to communicate has been discussed in Chapter 6 and should have been developed over the years. This will now become a vital tool to promote your vision to the rest of the staff and the governors. You will need to inspire others, but at the same time maintain a sense of reality, an awareness of the level of commitment of the others and of other pressures which they have to cope with.

Democratic leadership takes note of the opinions of all of those in the group. Tests have shown that it promotes cooperation between the members of the team, (Lewin, Lippitt and White, 1939) and greater productivity (Sayles, 1986) both cited in Gross (1987). As a head, you will need the cooperation of the staff if the school is to work towards its mission with any success. Listening and responding to the thoughts, worries and ideas of the rest of the staff is the way towards gaining that cooperation.

As a leader you will need to manage the changes that lead to development. Some of these may be changes to your own perceptions. Some will be changes you wish others to make. Knowing the staff is the key to making changes. Find out who does agree with what you want. Find out who are the key players amongst the staff. Identify the difficult, reluctant movers. Then work through the changes with measured steps. If you used the opportunities offered to you as a deputy, you will have increased your skills and abilities to handle people, learned to work with them or around them, and developed the ability to read situations wisely and respond tactfully. It is easier to make changes when everyone is pulling in the same direction and it is more likely that those changes will be maintained and not manipulated.

There will have been frequent opportunities during your time as a deputy when you were able to begin developing these abilities both as a manager and as a leader.

- List the skills and abilities you need to have to begin a career as a head.
- Identify the skills and abilities you already possess, through your experience as a team leader or curriculum coordinator.
- Identify the skills and abilities you are currently gaining, through new responsibilities as a deputy head.
- Identify areas you have yet to address. You can then add these areas of need to your professional development plan and possibly build them into your appraisal programme.

The skills and abilities you are gaining as a deputy head will be vital to your success as a head. It is therefore important that you acquire, practise and develop as many of them as you can while you have the chance to do so with support.

On your appointment as a head you will immediately become the principal manager of the school. You will be in control of what goes on, particularly of the financial and administrative aspects of the school. You will manage the curriculum, the children and the staff. Leadership depends on your enthusiasm and commitment, and your ability to communicate these to others and to inspire them to greater things. Then you will also be the leader of the school.

In an interview in *Director* magazine in November 1988, John Adair, former Chair of Leadership studies at the University of Surrey, claimed

> *you can be appointed a manager, but you're not a leader until your appointment is 'ratified' in the hearts and minds of those who work for you.*

Conclusion

What does the future hold?

The many changes in the education system during the late 1980s and early 1990s dramatically changed the role of the deputy head in the primary school. The role is likely to change even further in the years to come. It is up to those currently holding these posts to ensure that changes are for the better.

Even more importantly, it is up to us to ensure that the role continues to exist. The role must continue to have demonstrable and clearly defined differences from the roles carried out by any one else in the school.

Job descriptions should reflect these differences and should contain clear references to more senior management roles and responsibilities.

Heads should delegate authority along with responsibility, and respect the contributions made by their deputy to the overall running and development of the school.

The role of the deputy should be given the level of professionalism and commitment it deserves by those who accept the position.

Make the most of your time as a deputy head. Learn from it all you need to take the step into headship, if that is your ultimate goal. And when you are a head never forget what you have learnt and what you would like to have learned, during your time as a deputy head.

Further reading

Books

Gross, R D (1987) *Psychology: the Science of Mind and Behaviour*. London: Hodder and Stoughton.

Holly, P and **Southworth, G** (1989) *The Developing School*. Lewes: Falmer Press.

Kennedy, C (1991) *Guide to the Management Gurus*. London: Century Business.

Nias, J (1987) 'One finger, one thumb: a case study of the deputy head's part in the leadership of a nursery/infant school', in **Southworth, G** (ed) *Readings in School Management*. Lewes: Falmer Press.

Playfoot, D, **Skelton, M** and **Southworth, G** (1989) *The Primary School Management Book*. London: MGP/Collins

Southworth, G and **Lofthouse, B** (1990) *The Study of Primary Education: a Source Book – (2nd edition) Vol. 3, School Organisation and Management*. Lewes: Falmer Press.

Stoner, J A F and **Freeman, R E** (1989) *Management* (4th edition). Eaglewood Cliffs: Prentice Hall.

West, N (1992) *Primary Headship, Management and the Pursuit of Excellence: a school-based development guide for headship teams in primary schools*. Harlow: Longman.

Whitaker, P (1983) *The Primary Head*. Oxford: Heinemann Educational Books Ltd.

Young, P (1985) 'Implications for management in education', in **Reynolds, D** (ed) *Studying School Effectiveness*. Lewes: Falmer Press.

Reports

DfEE (1995) *School Teachers' Pay and Conditions Document 1995.* London: HMSO

OFSTED (1995) *New Framework for the Inspection of Schools.* London: HMSO

Journals

Coulson, A and **Cox, M** (1975) 'What do deputies do?' *Education 3–13,* 3, 2, *100–103.*

Purvis, J R and **Dennison, W F** (1993) 'Primary school deputy headship – has ERA and LMS changed the job?' *Education 3–13,* 21, 2, *15–21.*

Index

Academic development 34

Applications 37–38

Authority 16, 26, 27, 61

Confidentiality 22, 44

CV 31–32

Governors 9, 28, 41, 51, 55, 57

Interviews 37–39

Job specification 13–14

Leader 2, 3, 55, 57–60

Manager 51, 55, 56–57, 60

OFSTED 2,60

Partnership 15–16,18–19

Pay and conditions of service 4–5

Professional development 5, 12, 20, 23–25, 26, 31

Teaching commitment 11

Also available from pfp

Each **Primary File Guide** deals with an issue of current and lasting concern to teachers. Thoroughly researched and written in a clear, concise style, the series includes the following titles.

The Primary File Guide to... School Development Plans

Martin Skelton and David Playfoot

School development plans are now an everyday part of running a school. They help to ensure that real progress is made and that staff, the management team, governors and OFSTED-trained inspectors are all aware of the priorities and plans. This guide identifies what school development plans really are and what they can do for your school. It gives the six key areas for planning and discusses the writing of targets and the identification of success criteria and priorities. This is, essentially, a practical guide and so shows you how to make the most of development plans in your school.

isbn 1 874050 24 4

The Primary File Guide to... Surviving as an NQT

Julie Jennings

Being an NQT can be a trying and demanding experience. The pressures of a new job, combined with the everyday demands of the classroom, can be highly stressful. Julie Jennings provides the practical support every newly-qualified teacher needs. Written from personal experience, this guide will help you get through your first year of teaching with a little more confidence. It is also a valuable resource for experienced mentors and other teachers working alongside NQTs.

isbn 1 874050 27 9

Also available from pfp

The Primary File Guide to... Headship

Dr Geoff Southworth

The head of today's primary school has a massively demanding task involving the day-to-day running of a complex institution with responsibilities ranging from the minor to the very demanding. This guide identifies the key tasks of headship and suggests ways in which these can be fulfilled successfully. The book looks at the skills and qualities required by a good head and provides guidance on how to develop them. It also looks at how heads can and should influence a whole range of factors in a school – from ethos and teaching to working with staff and governors.

isbn 1 874050 28 7

The Primary File Guide to... Producing School Policies

Martin Skelton and David Playfoot

Policies are a vital part of creating an effective school, but there is little real help on how to produce and implement policies that actually work. This practical book provides the answer by covering all the key issues: What is a policy? Why does it matter? How to produce a policy. How to put it into practice. How to review and maintain its effectiveness.

isbn 1 874050 13 9

format – 64-80 pages, 130mm x 197mm